WASHINGTON'S

RULES OF CIVILITY

WASHINGTON'S

RULES OF CIVILITY

AND

DECENT BEHAVIOR
IN COMPANY AND CONVERSATION.

A PAPER

FOUND AMONG THE EARLY WRITINGS

BY

GEORGE WASHINGTON.

COPIED FROM THE ORIGINAI WITH LITERAL EXACTNESS,
AND EDITED WITH NOTES

J. M. TONER, M. D.

ISBN: 978-93-5128-963-0(HB)

First Published in 1888
Indian Reprint in 2017

Published by

Kalpaz Publications
C-30, Satyawati Nagar,
Delhi – 110052
E-mail: kalpaz@hotmail.com
Website: kalpazpublications.com
Ph.: +91-9212142040

PREFACE.

THE unceasing desire of the public to learn more and more of the life and character of General Washington induces me to publish entire, and for the first time with literal exactness, his "Rules of Civility & Decent Behaviour in Company and Conversation."

They were written by him at about the age of 13, and, with the exception of some school exercises, are the earliest of his productions, in the order of time, which have been preserved. It is proper, too, that their publication should precede that of his Diaries and Journals, taken by me from the original manuscript and arranged in chronological order with notes, which are now nearly ready for the press.

The

The first of the series Washington himself entitles, "A Journal of my Journey over the Mountains begun 11 March 1747–8." It will be seen from this date that he was then but 16 years and one month old.

J. M. T.

INTRODUCTION.

WHILE the authorship of these rules or maxims of civility and decent behavior in company is not positively known, it may be inferred with reasonable certainty. They are found in the handwriting of George Washington when he was quite a youth. His age is inferred from the date 1745 on one of the pages of the copy book in which these maxims are written. The first impression on reading them is likely to be (considering their merit and his age at the period of their production) that they were copied by him from some work on etiquette as an exercise or study. While this may be the fact, my investigation of the matter does not sustain such a view. Anxious

to

to settle definitely the question of authorship, I made a very thorough search through all the treatises on these topics printed before 1745, contained in the Library of Congress, but without discovering anything either identical with, or at all similar to them, in form or arrangement. The method adopted by the early writers on these subjects was to treat them by chapters, as "on etiquette at Court," "in the parlor," "at a ball," "at a dinner," &c. But nowhere do I find the whole subject matter of civility and behavior in company reduced to a single series of comprehensive maxims as they are in this paper. These rules of good behavior in Washington's own handwriting were examined, and fifty-seven of them published by Sparks in his Life and Writings of Washington, Vol. II, p. 412, but with numerous verbal alterations and considerable omissions

omissions of the subject-matter. I have transcribed, and here give to the public, these maxims complete and with literal exactness, just as they were recorded by Washington, believing that the reader will prefer to have them as they were left by him with all their peculiarities, without any of the polishings of an editor. Mr. Sparks says: "The source from which they were derived is not mentioned." In another place he states that they are "drawn from miscellaneous sources," and again he speaks of them as "these rules thus early selected and adopted as his guide." Irving, in his "Life of Washington," speaking of these rules of civility, says: "It was probably his intercourse with them [the Fairfaxes] and his ambition to acquit himself well in their society, that set him upon compiling a code of morals and manners, which still exists in manuscript in his own handwriting."

handwriting." Having searched in vain to find these rules in print, I feel justified, considering all the circumstances, in assuming that they were compiled by George Washington himself when a school-boy.

But while making this claim it is proper to state that nearly all the principles incorporated and injunctions given in these 110 maxims had been enunciated over and over again in the various works on good behavior and manners prior to this compilation and for centuries observed in polite society. It will be noticed that, while the spirit of these maxims is drawn chiefly from the social life of Europe, yet, as formulated here, they are as broad as civilization itself, though a few of them are especially applicable to society as it then existed in America, and, also, that but few refer to women. The latter fact may possibly

possibly be accounted for by the youth of the author.

The cardinal principles essential to the foundation of good manners are here assembled in so orderly a manner as to constitute a complete code of regulations for the development of habits, morals, and manners in young persons, and they were thoroughly mastered by Washington, and doubtless had great influence in the formation of his own noble character. These particular rules of civility and good behavior, although quaint, must always possess peculiar historical interest, because of their origin as well as for their intrinsic merits. It is therefore hoped that the publication of a true and complete copy of them from the original manuscript may prove not only gratifying to American pride but be of benefit to the growing youth of our country.

J. M. T.

Rules of Civility & Decent Behaviour

In Company and Conversation.

[The text following is an exact copy from the original manuscript, having been carefully compared with and corrected therefrom, even where errors or omissions are obvious.]

1st EVERY Action done in Company, ought to be with Some Sign of Respect, to those that are Present.[1]

2d When in Company, put not your Hands to any Part of the Body, not usualy Discovered.

3d Shew Nothing to your Friend that may affright him.

4th In the Presence of Others sing not to yourself with a humming Noise, nor Drum, with your Fingers or Feet.

5th IF YOU Cough, Sneeze, Sigh, or Yawn, do it not Loud, but Privately; and Speak not

(1) The thoughtful reader will recognize in this rule the germ and spirit of all rules of civility and the universal key to good behavior.

in

in your Yawning, but put Your handkerchief or Hand before your face and turn aside

6th SLEEP not when others Speak, Sit not when others stand, Speak not when you Should hold your Peace, walk not on when others Stop

7th PUT not off your Cloths in the presence of Others, nor go out your Chamber half Drest

8th AT PLAY and at Fire its Good manners to give Place to the last Commer, and affect not to Speak Louder than ordenary.

9th SPIT not in the Fire, nor Stoop low before it neither Put your Hands into the Flames to warm them, nor Set your Feet upon the Fire especially if there be meat before it(2)

(2) From early colonial times the kitchen of American houses had always a fire in it to which the stranger when fatigued, cold, or hungry, was admitted to hospitality without ceremony.

In new settlements the kitchen was the first room built, and it was generally of considerable dimension, with a large open fireplace, in which in cold weather was kept a blazing wood-fire for both use and comfort.

10th When you Sit down, Keep your Feet firm and Even, without putting one on the other or Crossing them

11th SHIFT not yourself in the Sight of others nor Gnaw your nails.

12th SHAKE not the head, Feet, or Legs rowl not the Eys, lift not one eyebrow higher than the other wry not the mouth, and bedew no mans face with your Spittle, by appr . . . . r him . . . . you Speak.(3)

Down the wide-throated chimney from a cross pole hung chains and crooks on which at times were suspended the heavier pots and kettles. And from the wide chimney jamb swung the freighted crane over an ample stone hearth, above which, and in front of the fire, revolved the loaded spit and sat at certain times of the day many implements of cookery. Yet this room, even when there were others, was nevertheless almost exclusively used, by the frontier farmers, as the family and guest assembly and dining hall. In the South, where planting was more extensively followed and colored servants did the work, there was usually an "Out Kitchen," often detached entirely from the mansion house, where the cooking was done. In these cases the family sitting apartment was often the dining room. The cooking stove and cooking range had not then been invented.

To a people living in a sparsely settled country engaged in subduing the forest and defending themselves against the savage Indian, such as ours were in early colonial times, the 9th rule had an aptness not now apparent.

(3) The book in which Washington wrote the rules of civility

13th

13th KILL no Vermin as Fleas, lice ticks &c in the Sight of Others, if you See any filth or thick Spittle put your foot Dexteriously upon it if it be upon the Cloths of your Companions, Put it off privately, and if it be upon your own Cloths return Thanks to him who puts it off[4]

has been damaged by mice, which ate away a portion of the back and some of the lower end of all the leaves, which in places has involved one or more lines or parts of lines in the text. Rule 12 and all other rules written at the bottom of any of the pages have been nearly destroyed. Every word and letter, however, that remains has been copied, and are here given.

(4) The matters treated of in this rule are not agreeable subjects to discuss, yet, as society existed when they were formulated. such questions forced themselves upon the attention of the people.

The flea was, in early times, and indeed still is, a great pest. In certain localities, and particularly in warm, sandy countries, or wherever domestic animals are harbored in or about dwellings, small as the flea is he makes himself felt. There is a township, in North Carolina, named Flea-hill. The California Sand-hills, too, are noted for being infested with these troublesome insects. The existence of lice is usually ascribed to neglect of personal cleanliness, and to a great extent this is true; yet gentlemen who have served in the Army—officers as well as common soldiers—know how difficult it is where men are crowded together, to prevent their becoming troublesome.

Spitting on the floor, which was deemed an offence 150 years ago, is a vice which still exists even at the present day. The method suggested for hiding the nuisance was in its spirit considerate and praiseworthy. Bare floors were then the universal custom ; the floor-mat came slowly into use, and carpets are of still later date.

It is probable that when these rules were compiled there were but very few carpeted rooms in the American colonies, and the modern bath-room and tub were almost unknown.

14th TURN not your Back to others especially in Speaking, Jog not the Table or Desk on which Another reads or writes, lean not upon any one.

15th KEEP your Nails clean and Short, also your Hands and Teeth Clean, yet without Shewing any great Concern for them

16th DO not Puff up the Cheeks, Loll not out the tongue rub the Hands, or beard, thrust out the lips, or bite them or keep the Lips too open or too Close.

17th BE no Flatterer, neither Play with any that delights not to be Play'd Withal.

18th READ no Letters, Books, or Papers in Company but when there is a Necessity for the doing of it you must ask leave: come not near the Books or Writings of Another so as to read them unless desired or give your opinion of them unask'd also look not nigh when another is writing a Letter

19th. let your Countenance be pleasant but in Serious Matters Somewhat grave

20th. The Gestures of the Body must be Suited to the discourse you are upon

21st. Reproach none for the Infirmaties of Nature, nor Delight to Put them that have in mind thereof.

22d. Shew not yourself glad at the Misfortune of another though he were your enemy

23d. When you see a Crime punished, you may be inwardly Pleased; but always shew Pity to the Suffering Offender.

. . . . too much at any Publick[5]

. . . .

25th. SUPERFLUOUS Complements and all Affec[ta]tion of Ceremony are to be avoided, yet where due they are not to be Neglected

26th. IN PULLING off your Hat to Persons

(5) **Rule 24 was written at the bottom of the book where it has been damaged, as stated in Note 3.**

of

of Distinction, as Noblemen, Justices, Churchmen &c make a Reverence, bowing more or less according to the Custom of the Better Bred, and Quality of the Persons Amongst your equals expect not always that they Should begin with you first, but to Pull off the Hat when there is no need is Affectation, in the Manner of Saluting and resaluting in words keep to the most usual Custom.

27th TIS ill manners to bid one more eminent than yourself be covered as well as not to do it to whom it's due Likewise he that makes too much haste to Put on his hat does not well, yet he ought to Put it on at the first, or at most the Second time of being ask'd; now what is herein Spoken, of Qualification in behaviour in Saluting, ought also to be observed in taking of Place, and Sitting down for ceremonies without Bounds is troublesome.

28th IF ANY one come to Speak to you while you are are Sitting Stand up tho he be your Inferiour, and when you Present Seats let it be to every one according to his Degree.

29th WHEN you meet with one of Greater Quality than yourself, Stop, and retire especially if it be at a Door or any Straight place to give way for him to Pass

30th IN walking the highest Place in most Countrys Seems to be on the right hand therefore Place yourself on the left of him whom you desire to Honour: but if three walk together the middle Place is the most Honourable the wall is usually given to the most worthy if two walk together.

31st IF any one far Surpasses others, either in age Estate, or Merit, . . . would give Place to a meaner than himself . . . .

the

the one ought not to except it, So . . . .
it above once or twice.[6]

32d. TO one that is your equal, or not much inferior you are to give the chief Place in your Lodging and he to who 'tis offered ought at the first to refuse it but at the Second to accept though not without acknowledging his own unworthiness

33d. THEY that are in Dignity or in office have in all places Preceedency but whilst they are Young they ought to respect those that are their equals in Birth or other Qualitys, though they have no Publick charge.

34th. IT is good Manners to prefer them to whom we speak before ourselves especially if they be above us with whom in no Sort we ought to begin.

35th. LET your Discourse with Men of Business be Short and Comprehensive.

(6) Rule 31 occurs at the bottom of the manuscript where it has been injured; the words remaining are given.

36th ARTIFICERS & Persons of low Degree ought not to use many ceremonies to Lords, or Others of high Degree but Respect and highly Honour them, and those of high Degree ought to treat them with affibility & Courtesie, without Arrogancy

37th IN Speaking to men of Quality do not lean nor Look them full in the Face, nor approach too near them at lest Keep a full Pace from them.

38th IN visiting the Sick, do not Presently play the Physicion if you be not Knowing therein.

39th IN writing or Speaking, give to every Person his due Title According to his Degree & the Custom of the Place.

40th STRIVE not with your Superiers in argument, but always Submit your Judgment to others with Modesty

41st Undertake not to Teach your equal in the art himself Professes; it flavours of arrogancy.

. . . . curtesie be proper to the
. . . . Dignity of his place
. . . . t yr same with a
. . . . Clown and a Prince.(7)

43d DO not express Joy before one sick or in pain for that contrary Passion will aggravate his Misery

44th When a man does all he can though it Succeeds not well blame not him that did it.

45th BEING to advise or reprehend any one, consider whether it ought to be in publick or in Private; presently, or at Some other time in what terms to do it & in reproving Shew no Signs of Cholar but do it with all Sweetness and Mildness

(7) Rule 42 was written on that part of the original manuscript destroyed by mice.

46th

46th Take all Admonitions thankfully in what Time or Place Soever given but afterwards not being culpable take a Time or Place Convenient to let him him know it that gave them.

..7th MOCK not nor Jest at anything of Importance break no Jest that are Sharp Biting and if you Deliver anything witty and Pleasent abtain from Laughing thereat yourself.

48th WHEREIN wherein you reprove Another be unblameable yourself; for example is more prevalent than Precepts

49. USE no Reproachfull Language against any one neither Curse nor Revile

..0th BE not hasty to believe flying Reports to the Disparagement of any

51st WEAR not your Cloths, foul, unript or Dusty but See they be Brush'd once every day

day at least and take heed that you approach not to any Uncleaness

52^{d} IN your Apparel be Modest and endeavour to accomodate Nature, rather than to procure Admiration keep to the Fashion of your equals Such as are Civil and orderly with respect to Times and Places

53^{d} RUN not in the Streets, neither go too slowly nor with Mouth open go not Shaking y^{r} Arms . . . .
not upon the toes, nor in a Dancing, ... [8]

54th PLAY not the Peacock, looking everywhere about you, to See if you be well Deck't, if your Shoes fit well if your Stockings Sit neatly, and Cloths handsomely.

55th EAT not in the Streets, nor in ye House, out of Season.

56th ASSOCIATE yourself with Men of

(8) Rule 53 in part destroyed by mice.

good

good Quality if you Esteem your own Reputation; for 'tis better to be alone than in bad Company.

57th IN walking up and Down in a House, only with One in Company if he be Greater than yourself, at the first give him the Right hand and Stop not till he does and be not the first that turns, and when you do turn let it be with your face towards him, if he be a Man of Great Quality, walk not with him Cheek by Jowl but Somewhat behind him; but yet in Such a Manner that he may easily Speak to you.

58th LET your Conversation be without Malice or Envy, for 'tis a Sign of a Tractable and Commendable Nature: & in all Causes of Passion admit Reason to Govern

59th NEVER express anything unbecoming, nor Act agst ye Rules of Moral before your inferiours

60th

60th. BE not immodest in urging your Friends to Discover a Secret.

61st. UTTER not base and frivilous things amongst grave and Learn'd Men nor very Difficult Questions or Subjects, among the Ignorant or things hard to be believed, Stuff not your Discourse with Sentences amongst your Betters nor Equals

62d. SPEAK not of doleful Things in a Time of Mirth or at the Table; Speak not of Melancholy Things as Death and Wounds, and if others Mention them Change if you can the Discourse tell not your Dreams, but to your intimate Friend

63d. A MAN ought not to value himself of his Atchievements or rare Qua- . . . . les Virtue or Kindred(9).

. . . .

(9) Rule 63 destroyed from causes stated.

64th. BREAK not a Jest where none take pleasure in mirth Laugh not aloud, nor at all without Occasion, deride no man's Misfortune, tho' there seem to be Some cause

65th. SPEAK not injurious Words neither in Jest nor Earnest Scoff at none although they give Occasion

66th. BE not forward but friendly and Courteous; the first to Salute hear and answer & be not Pensive when it's a time to converse.

67th. DETRACT not from others neither be excessive in Commanding.

68th. GO not not thither, where you know not, whether you Shall be Welcome or not. Give not Advice whth being Ask'd & when desired do it briefly

69th. IF two contend together take not the part of either unconstrained, and be not obsti-

nate

nate in your Opinion, in Things indiferent be of the Major side.

70th. REPREHEND not the imperfections of others for that belongs to Parents Masters and Superiours.

71st. GAZE not on the marks or blemishes of Others and ask not how they came. What you may Speak in Secret to your Friend deliver not before others

72d. SPEAK not in an unknown Tongue in Company but in your own Language and that as those of Quality do and not as ye. Vulgar; Sublime matters treat Seriously.

73d. THINK before you Speak pronounce not imperfectly nor bring out your Words too hastily but orderly and Distinctly

74th. WHEN Another Speaks be attentive your Self and disturb not the Audience if any hesitate in his Words help him not nor Prompt him without desired, Interrupt him not, nor Answer him till his Speech be ended

75th IN the midst of Discourse ask . . . . . but if you Perceive any Stop because of . . . [10] to Proceed: IF a Person of Quality comes in while your Conversing its handsome to Repeat what was said before

76th WHILE you are talking, Point not with your Finger at him of Whom you Discourse nor Approach too near him to whom you talk especially to his face

77th TREAT with men at fit Times about Business & Whisper not in the Company of Others

78th MAKE no Comparisons and if any of the Company be Commended for any brave act of Virtue, commend not another for the Same

(10) Rule 75 in part destroyed.

79th BE not apt to relate News if you know not the truth thereof. IN Discoursing of things you Have heard Name not your Author always A Secret Discover not.

80th BE not Tedious in Discourse or in reading unless you find the Company pleased therewith

81st BE not Curious to Know the Affairs tof Others neither approach to those that Speak in Private

82d UNDERTAKE not what you cannot Perform but be Carefull to keep your Promise

83d WHEN you deliver a matter do it without Passion & with Discretion, however mean ye Person be you do it too

84th WHEN your Superiours talk to any Body hearken not neither Speak nor Laugh

85th IN Company of these of Higher Quality than yourself Speak not till you are ask'd

a

a Question then Stand upright put of your Hat & Answer in few words

86. IN Disputes, be not so Desirous to Overcome as not to give Liberty to each one to deliver his Opinion and Submit to ye Judgment of ye Major Part especially if they are Judges of the Dispute.

87th . . . . as becomes a Man Grave
. . . . Settled and attentive
. . . . dict not at every
. . . . turn what others Say[11]

88th BE not tedious in Discourse, make not many Digressions, nor repeat often the Same manner of Discourse

89th Speak not Evil of the absent for it is unjust

90th BEING Set at meat Scratch not neither Spit Cough or blow your Nose except there's a Necessity for it

(11) Rule 87 is partly destroyed.

91st MAKE no Shew of taking great Delight in your Victuals, Feed not with Greediness; cut your Bread with a Knife, lean not on the Table neither find fault with what you Eat

92d TAKE no Salt or cut Bread with your Knife Greasy.

93d ENTERTAINING any one at table it is decent to present him wt meat, Undertake not to help others undesired by ye Master

9. 4th IF you Soak bread in the Sauce let it be no more than what you put in your Mouth at a time and blow not your broth at Table but Stay till Cools of it Self

95th PUT not your meat to your Mouth with your Knife in your hand neither Spit forth the Stones of any fruit Pye upon a Dish nor cast anything under the table

96th IT'S unbecoming to Stoop much to

ones

ones Meat Keep your Fingers clean & when foul wipe them on a Corner of your Table Napkin

.. 7th PUT not another bit into your Mouth til the former be Swallowed let not your Morsels be too big for the jowls

98th DRINK not nor talk with your mouth full neither Gaze about you while you are a Drinking

99th DRINK not too leisurely nor yet too hastily. Before and after Drinking wipe your Lips breath not then or Ever with too Great a Noise, for its uncivil

100th CLEANSE not your teeth with the Table Cloth Napkin Fork or Knife but if Others do it let it be done wt a Pick Tooth

101st RINCE not your Mouth in the Presence of Others

102d IT is out of use to call upon the Company

pany

pany often to Eat nor need you Drink to others every Time you Drink

103d IN Company of your Betters be not . . . . than they are lay not your Arm but ar . (12)

104th IT belongs to ye Chiefest in Company to unfold his Napkin and fall to Meat first, But he ought then to Begin in time & to Dispatch with Dexterity that ye Slowest may have time allowed him

105th BE not Angry at Table whatever happens & if you have reason to be so, Shew it not but on a Chearfull Countenance especially if there be Strangers for good Humour makes one Dish of Meat a Feast

106th SET not yourself at ye upper . . . . of ye Table but if it be your Due or that ye Master of ye house will have it so, Contend not least you Should Trouble ye company.(13)

(12) Rule 103 in part destroyed by the causes stated.
(13) Rule 106. A blank . . . . space exists after the word upper where it is presumed the word end was intended.

107th IF others talk at Table be attentive but talk not with Meat in your Mouth

108th WHEN you Speak of God or his Atributes, let it be Seriously & . . . . Reverence. Honour & obey your Natural Parents altho they be Poor

109th LET your Recreations be Manfull not Sinfull.

110th LABOUR to keep alive in your Breast that Little Spark of Celestial fire called Conscience.[14]

(14) This closing maxim or injunction, the observance of which is so important in the make up of a man's character, is thus most appropriately placed at the end, and its choice for that place is peculiarly characteristic of Washington's style. Throughout all his writings he is especially noted for his good taste and apt allusions to his subject in the opening and closing of his letters and communications, and the example here given is a proof that this talent was not wanting even in his earliest youth.

FINIS.